Developing Character When It Counts

A Program for Teaching Character in the Classroom

Grades 2–3

Written by Barbara Allman
Illustrated by C.A. Nobens

"CHARACTER COUNTS!" and "Six Pillars of Character" are service marks of the CHARACTER COUNTS! Coalition, a project of the Josephson Institute.

FS119101 Developing Character When It Counts Grades 2-3
All rights reserved—Printed in the U.S.A.
Copyright © 1999 Frank Schaffer Publications
23740 Hawthorne Blvd.
Torrance, CA 90505

Table of Contents

Introduction

by Michael Josephson, President, CHARACTER COUNTS!℠ Coalition

Character is what a person is inside. Our character is revealed by how we act when we think no one else is looking. It is how we treat people who we think cannot help or hurt us. A person of character has good ethical values that distinguish right from wrong and a strong commitment to do what is right even when it is inconvenient, uncomfortable, or personally costly. Character, in short, is moral strength.

Good character does not develop spontaneously. Rather, it is the result of conscientious efforts to instill and reinforce ethical values in a way that makes them second nature. This sense of right and wrong is often referred to as the conscience. Conscience is the moral compass of character.

This book is organized around the Six Pillars of Character℠, a character development framework developed by the CHARACTER COUNTS!℠ Coalition, an alliance of hundreds of leading educational, youth-serving, and community organizations dedicated to strengthening the character of youth. The Six Pillars of Character℠ are trustworthiness, respect, responsibility, fairness, caring, and citizenship.

Developing Character When It Counts is divided into six sections, with each dedicated to a specific value. The book examines the nature and importance of character through writing assignments, discussions, and hands-on activities.

What Is Trustworthiness?

A person who is trustworthy

lives with integrity, and is

honest, reliable, and loyal.

Trustworthiness

Teach your students the importance of being trustworthy.

Circle of Trust

Brainstorm with your students about the key words in the definition on the left side of this page. On chart paper, write the word *trustworthiness* in a circle in the center of the page. Then draw four large petals around the circle, each with one of the following words: *integrity*, *honesty*, *reliablity*, and *loyalty*. Encourage the children to volunteer their ideas for each petal. Write their ideas on the appropriate petals. Below are some ideas to emphasize in each category.

Trustworthiness: Key Ideas

Integrity: To have integrity means to stand up for your beliefs and live by your principles, no matter what others say. It is having the courage to do what is right and to try new things even when they are difficult, costly, or you might fail. If you have integrity, you do not do anything that you know is wrong, and you do not lose heart if you fail.

Honesty: To be honest is to tell the truth. It also means to be sincere, forthright, and candid. An honest person is not sneaky, and does not lie, cheat, or steal.

Reliability: To be reliable is to keep your promises and be dependable. A reliable person returns what is borrowed, pays debts, and is on time.

Loyalty: To have loyalty is to stand by your family, friends, school, and country. A loyal person is a good friend who would never betray a trust, let friends hurt themselves, or ask a friend to do anything wrong.

Trustworthiness

Share a poem about trustworthiness.

Rebecca's Afterthought
by Elizabeth Turner

Yesterday, Rebecca Mason,
    In the parlor by herself,
Broke a handsome china basin,
    Placed upon the mantel shelf.

Quite alarmed, she thought of going
    Very quietly away,
Not a single person knowing,
    Of her being there that day.

But Rebecca recollected
    She was taught deceit to shun;
And the moment she reflected,
    Told her mother what was done;

Who commended her behavior,
Loved her better, and forgave her.

Role-play

Invite the children to role-play the action in the poem with a partner. Have one partner play Rebecca and one play her parent. Review the poem's action. Guide the children in inventing dialogue to go with their dramatizations of the story. Having a verbal "script" of what to say in a situation can help children act appropriately in real-life situations.

Character Report Card

Ask the children to help you make a list of things they know about Rebecca in the poem. Is she trustworthy? Does she make mistakes? Is she honest? If your students were to make a report card for her, what grades would they give her in those categories?

Report Card for Rebecca | Honesty A | Trust A | Mistakes A

FS119101 Developing Character When It Counts

"Be slow to fall into friendship, but when you have, be firm and constant in that friendship."—Socrates

Friendship Is a Golden Thread

Friendship wristbands will serve to remind your students of the importance of having and being a trustworthy friend. Children can make a variety of colorful beads and string them on gold elastic thread. Each bead can represent a friend or other trustworthy person. Just as the people in our lives are all different, so is each bead. But they are all tied together with the golden thread of friendship.

Demonstrate how to make beads from magazine pages by cutting a page into strips approximately one inch wide. Fold one end of a strip over the middle of a pencil and glue the strip to itself. Then squeeze glue all along the strip. Place your hands on either end of the pencil and gently roll it, rolling up the strip into a bead. Carefully slip the bead off the pencil and let it dry.

String the beads using a bobby pin as a needle. Handmade paper beads may be alternated with large plastic beads. Tie the ends together to form a friendship wristband.

Trustworthy Friend Kit

Provide the following items for each child to make a Trustworthy Friend Kit.

- Copy of *Trustworthy Friend Kit* (page 7)
- A business-size envelope
- Piece of colorful tape
- Bandage
- Button
- Candy heart
- Word card with the word *truth*
- Small eraser
- Wrapped candy mint

Use the kit as a discussion starter. Then encourage the children to take their kits home and discuss with family members what each item represents. As a homework assignment, have each student bring in another small item for his or her kit and explain its meaning to the class.

Trustworthiness

Literature helps children learn important lessons about character.

Literature List

The following books give children a look at the importance of being trustworthy.

The Adventures of Obadiah by Brinton Turkle (Viking, 1988). Obadiah stretches the truth so often that his family doesn't believe him when he tells them about his real experiences at the sheep-shearing fair.

The Empty Pot by Demi (Henry Holt, 1990). Ping, a young boy, has the courage to tell the truth to the Emperor, and is chosen to succeed him.

Jamaica's Find by Juanita Havill (Houghton Mifflin, 1986). Jamaica finds a stuffed toy that is hard to part with, but when she returns it, she gains a friend.

Beauty and the Beast retold by Jan Brett (Clarion, 1989). Beauty keeps her word to the Beast, and lives happily ever after.

Abraham Lincoln

by Ingri & Edgar Parin D'Aulaire
(Dell, 1939, 1957)

This classic picture book contains many stories about Honest Abe that are worth sharing with children. Read the book aloud in installments over a few day's time. Children will hear how Abe walked three miles to give a woman back the money he had mistakenly overcharged her. They will also learn that Lincoln paid back all his debts when his partner mismanaged their store.

Have children contribute to a class list of characteristics they think made Lincoln a good president. Ask them to give examples of times when Lincoln demonstrated these characteristics.

Give each child a piece of drawing paper cut from a brown paper grocery bag. Crumpling the paper will give it an antique, rustic look. Ask the children to draw and label one of Lincoln's qualities. Assemble the drawings in a class book with brown poster board covers cut in a log cabin shape. Title the book "Trustworthy Abe." Place the book in your classroom library for the children to read.

FS119101 Developing Character When It Counts

Trustworthiness Detectives

Tell your students to imagine they are news reporters. Their job was to find the world's most trustworthy friend and follow that person around for a week. Together, make a class list of things they might have seen this trustworthy person do or say.

Then, have your reporters use the ideas on the class list to write about this imaginary person, describing his or her actions and habits. Their reports must answer this question: What makes a trustworthy friend?

Class List
World's Most
Trustworthy Person
• Tells the truth.
• Keeps a promise.
• Protects others.
• Sticks up for a friend.
• Stands up for what's right.

> In front of their friends, Amy said something about Megan that hurt her feelings. Later, when they were alone, Megan told Amy how hurt she was.

> Dan promised to go bike riding with Ben after school. When another friend wanted to play basketball with Dan after school, Dan said not today, because he had to meet Ben.

> Ally made a bead necklace for her friend Stephanie's birthday. She showed the necklace to Jared and asked him to keep it a secret. Jared told Stephanie about the necklace.

Developing Trust

Write the following ideas on separate index cards and distribute each to a small group of children. Ask the groups to read their cards aloud and then tell whether they think the friends in each situation showed trustworthiness.

1. In front of their friends, Amy said something about Megan that hurt her feelings. Later, when they were alone, Megan told Amy how hurt she was.

2. Dan promised to go bike riding with Ben after school. When another friend wanted to play basketball with Dan after school, Dan said that he couldn't because he had to meet Ben.

3. Ally made a bead necklace for her friend Stephanie's birthday. She showed the necklace to Jared and asked him to keep it a secret. Jared told Stephanie about the necklace.

Trustworthy Friend Kit

Make a friendship kit to remind yourself of what it takes to be a trustworthy friend. Label an envelope "Friendship Kit" and decorate it. Place the things on this list inside the envelope. Cut out the list and put it in the friendship kit, too. Take your friendship kit home and tell your family what each thing in the kit stands for.

Be a Trustworthy Friend

Tape
Stick up for your friend.

Bandage
Never let a friend do anything to harm himself or herself.

Button
"Button your lips" and keep a secret for a friend.

Candy Heart
Have the courage to do the right thing.

Word Card: Truth
Remember to always speak the truth. Be honest and sincere with your friend.

Eraser
Everyone makes mistakes. Forgive a friend's mistakes.

Mint
A trustworthy friend is worth a mint.

Name ____

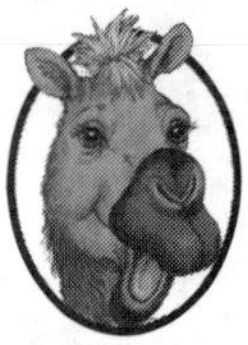

Being a Friend

Here is a picture of my friend ____________________ and me.

My Friend is a Good Friend

A Good Friend is My Friend

My friend __________________________ is a good friend because

____

____

____

I am a good friend because ______________________________________

____

____

____

Name _____

Lincoln and the General Store

There are many stories about Abraham Lincoln that tell what a trustworthy person he was. When he was a young man, Lincoln had a business partner named William Berry. They owned a general store together, but neither of the two men knew much about running a store. The store failed and then William Berry died. This left Lincoln with a huge debt to pay—over a thousand dollars. Abe had never made more than a few dollars a month, but he made up his mind to pay back all the money he owed. And he did, though it took him fifteen years to do it.

Trustworthiness means being reliable. This means keeping your promises and paying your debts. Tell how Lincoln was reliable.

_____

_____

_____

Trustworthiness means having integrity. This means having the courage to do what is right even when it is hard. Tell how Lincoln had integrity.

_____

_____

_____

FS119101 Developing Character When It Counts   reproducible   © Frank Schaffer Publications, Inc.

What Is Respect?

A respectful person lives by the Golden Rule, accepts others who are different, lives peacefully, and shows courtesy to all.

Respect

Children can learn respect for themselves and others.

Create a Rainbow of Respect

Give your students the opportunity to make a rainbow of respect for your classroom. Discuss the key ideas in the definition on the left side of this page, elaborating on them with the children. (Further explanation of key ideas is given below.) Then use bulletin board paper in four colors to construct a large rainbow for a bulletin board. Cut the four arcs to fit together. Before mounting the arcs on the board, divide the class into four groups and give each group an arc. Also assign each group a key idea: *Golden Rule*, *tolerance and acceptance*, *nonviolence*, or *courtesy*.

Have students use large letter templates to trace and color the letters of their key idea onto the arc. Direct the group to discuss the meaning of their key idea and write a list on a separate sheet of paper. For example, for *Golden Rule*, they might write *Treat others the way you would like to be treated* or *Respect other people's property*. When the groups are ready with their ideas, have them share the ideas with the class and make appropriate changes. Then have the groups use colorful markers to write these ideas on their arcs. Staple the arcs in a rainbow on a bulletin board titled "We Show."

Respect: Key Ideas

Golden Rule: Treat others the way you want to be treated. Be polite and courteous. Respect the freedom of others. Respect the property of others—take care of things you are allowed to use, and don't take property without permission.

Tolerance and acceptance: Respect others who are different from you. Listen to the point of view of others and try to understand. Don't judge people by their outside appearances.

Nonviolence: Solve disagreements peacefully, without violence. Deal with anger peacefully. Do not use physical force to show anger or to get what you want.

Courtesy: Use good manners. Be polite and courteous to everyone. Do not hurt others by embarassing them, putting them down, or insulting them.

Respect

Share some "Rules of Civility."

Showing Respect With Good Manners

Tell your students that good manners show respect for others. When George Washington was a boy he copied an English translation of the French Jesuits' "Rules of Civility" into ten pages of one of his notebooks. Share some of those rules of mannerly behavior with your students. Afterward, have a discussion about how we would say each rule today. Have the children make small notebooks titled "Rules of Civility" by stapling two or three sheets of writing paper between construction paper covers. Allow students to choose several rules to copy into their books, just as George Washington did.

Rules of Civility and Decent Behavior In Company and Conversation

- Shift not yourself in the sight of others nor gnaw your nails.
- Eat not in the streets, nor in ye house, out of season.
- If you cough, sneeze, sigh, or yawn do it not loud but privately; and speak not in your yawning, but put your handkerchief or hand before your face and turn aside.
- While you are talking, point not with your finger at him of whom you discourse nor approach too near him to whom you talk especially to his face.
- Drink not nor talk with your mouth full neither gaze about you while you are a-drinking.
- Turn not your back to others especially in speaking.
- Jog not the table or desk on which another reads or writes, lean not upon anyone.
- Keep your nails clean and short, also your hands and teeth clean yet without showing any great concern for them.
- If others talk at table be attentive but talk not with meat in your mouth.

Role-play

Offer children an opportunity to practice verbalizing polite phrases. Together, brainstorm a list of kind words. Write each one on a slip of paper and place the papers in a box. Have each child choose a partner and draw a phrase from the box. Partners must plan a dialogue using the phrase they selected and act out a situation where it would be used. Allow time for partners to develop their dialogues and rehearse them, then have everybody share theirs with the class.

Respect

Help students resolve conflicts peacefully.

Blueprint for a Peaceful Classroom

Teach children that conflicts are okay and that it is possible to resolve them without hurting someone with our actions or words. Write the following steps on chart paper as you discuss them with the children.

1. Take time out and cool off. If you need to express anger, do it in a way that won't hurt you or someone else.
2. Let both people state their views of the problem.
3. Let both people state how they feel. "I feel ___ when you ____ ."
4. Let both people state the problem again, this time from the other person's view.
5. Together, think of several ways to solve the problem.
6. Choose a solution that will make both people feel good.
7. Shake hands. Say something nice to the other person.

Tell the children that to have a peaceful classroom (and a peaceful world) people need to work at it and not give up when it gets hard. Have someone volunteer a conflict situation that happened at school and have two people role-play using the guidelines above to resolve the problem. Give children an opportunity at least once a week to practice this way. Post the guidelines in a prominent spot in the classroom so children can refer to them when confronted with a real-life situation.

Gandhi, King, and I

Martin Luther King Jr. was not the first person to use peaceful resistance instead of violence to create social change. The idea can be traced to Gandhi, Thoreau, and even Aesop. Share Aesop's fable "The Wind and the Sun" with your students by copying page 15 for them. The lesson of this fable is about the power of gentleness over force. Have your students compare Aesop's ideas with those of Martin Luther King Jr. Can they think of ways children today can use peaceful means with each other?

The Golden Rule

Explain the Golden Rule to your students. Tell them that the phrase "do unto others as you would have them do unto you" is a way of saying "treat other people as you would like them to treat you." Ask the children to tell about a time when someone treated them kindly or did something special for them. How did it make them feel? Point out that following the Golden Rule builds respect between people. Have students draw and label pictures of actions which demonstrate the Golden Rule. Display these drawings under the heading "The Golden Rule." For a special effect, cut the letters out of shiny gold paper.

Respect

"We must live together as brothers or perish together as fools." —Martin Luther King Jr.

Teaching Tolerance and Acceptance

Children benefit from having an opportunity to listen to the viewpoints of others. They can develop respect and empathy for others by coming to understand and share other people's feelings.

Pair up your students for this activity. The children can share with their partners ways they are alike and ways they are different. Prepare a chart with several questions to get the partners started. (See suggestions below.) Have the partners list something they both like and something they both dislike. Then have the partners share their results with the class.

What is your favorite school subject?

What is your favorite sport?

What do you like to do outside of school?

What do you like to eat for lunch?

What animals do you like?

What authors do you like?

What TV shows do you watch?

Reading Faces

Being aware of the body language and facial expressions of others can help children relate to others better. Read aloud a story in which a character faces fear, such as *Mandy* by Barbara D. Booth (Lothrop, Lee & Shepard Books, 1991) or *The Lighthouse Keeper's Daughter* by Arielle North Olson (Little, Brown, 1987). Ask several students to show with their faces and bodies how the character felt. They may frown, look wide-eyed, quiver, and so on. Ask: *How do people look when they are frightened or nervous?* Then have the group tell in words what behaviors they saw that told them the actors were nervous or scared.

Have the children look for magazine pictures of people wearing different facial expressions. They can cut them out and glue the pictures on a large sheet of bulletin board paper to make a display titled "I Know How You Feel." As a class, review the pictures and decide on how to label each one with a feeling, such as delighted, scared, shy, unhappy, or angry.

13

Respect

Literature can nurture empathy and respect for others.

Literature List

Use the following books to introduce children to important concepts related to respect—courtesy, nonviolence, and empathy.

Manners by Aliki (Greenwillow, 1990). This book gives a look at manners, good and bad, in many situations.

My Dream of Martin Luther King by Faith Ringgold (Crown, 1995). Tells the life story of Martin Luther King Jr., who used peaceful resistance to bring about social change.

Prize in the Snow by Bill Easterling (Little, Brown, 1994). A young boy changes his mind about trapping when his empathy for a starving rabbit induces him to feed the animal instead.

Peace Begins With You

by Katherine Scholes
(Sierra Club, 1989)

In clear and simple language, this book explores the concept of peace and explains how conflicts can be resolved in peaceful ways. It shows how the choices made by individuals are important to peace everywhere.

Discuss with the children why "peace is a better way." Together, make a class list of the ways the book mentions that children can be peacemakers.

Set aside a special area of a bulletin board to acknowledge students who are peacemakers. Cut a large prize medallion and ribbon from colored posterboard. Leave space on the medallion for name cards or photos of the week's winners. Every week, have the children nominate their classmates to receive the peacemaker's prize. They should tell the class what the nominees have done to deserve the prize. Post the names or photos of the winners on the board and acknowledge them with a group handshake or hug. Then sing together a song of peace, such as "It's a Small World" or "I'd Like to Teach the World to Sing."

The Sun and the Wind
by Aesop

Long ago, the Wind and Sun were having an argument about who was stronger. They decided to have a contest.

"Do you see that man walking along the road, wearing a cloak?" asked the Sun.

"Yes," answered the Wind.

"Let's see who can make him take off his cloak," said the Sun.

So the Wind and Sun agreed. First, the Wind tried. It began to blow. It blew harder and harder. But the more it blew, the tighter the man wrapped himself in his cloak.

Finally, the Wind said to the Sun, "I give up. You try."

The Sun began to smile warmly at the man. The man began to feel the warmth of the sun. The sun got brighter and brighter. The man felt warmer and warmer. Soon the man was sweating as he walked along the road. Feeling hot and tired, he sat down on a big rock and threw off his cloak.

Lesson: Gentleness can do what force cannot.

1. How did the Wind try to win the contest?

   _____

   _____

2. How did the Sun win the contest?

   _____

FS119101 Developing Character When It Counts   reproducible   © Frank Schaffer Publications, Inc.

Name _____

Peacemaker

Do you know someone who is a peacemaker? It might be someone you know at school or at home, or someone in the news. Draw a special Peacemaker Award in the box. Write to explain why the person deserves it.

**Peacemaker Award
Given To**

_____

For

_____

Date _____

Why this person deserves an award:

_____

_____

_____

_____

_____

_____

Responsibility

Help your students develop responsibility at home, at school, and in their community.

Being Responsible

Discuss with your students the key ideas in the definition on the right side of this page. (Ideas are expanded below.) On a chalkboard or chart paper, make three lists using students' ideas about responsibilities at home, at school, and in the community. Under each heading, ask the children to dictate their ideas on ways they can do their duties and be accountable.

Home	School	Community
Clean my room.	Keep my desk neat.	Pick up trash.
Help with the dishes.	Do my best work.	Obey traffic laws.
Feed the cat.	Put things where they belong.	Help my neighbors.

Responsibility: Key Ideas

Duty: Do your duty. Know what is expected of you. This means understanding your legal and moral obligations.

Accountability: This means you accept responsibility for the consequences of your choices. It is taking responsibility for the things you choose to do and the things you choose not to do. Before you act, think about what will happen to you or others. Do what you can to make things better. Don't look the other way when you can make a difference.

Excellence: Pursuing excellence means doing your best. It means persevering (not giving up). Be prepared. Work hard.

Self-control: Set goals that are realistic for yourself. Have a positive attitude. Act out of reason, not anger, revenge, or fear. Have self-discipline when it comes to your health, emotions, time, and money. Be self-reliant.

What Is Responsibility?

A person who is responsible meets the demands of duty, is accountable for the consequences of his or her choices, pursues excellence and exercises self-control.

Responsibility

Share a rhyme about responsibility.

Little Boy Blue
(Traditional)

Little Boy Blue, come blow your horn,
The sheep's in the meadow, the cow's in the corn.
But where is the little boy tending the sheep?
He's under the haycock fast asleep.
Will you wake him? No, not I,
For if I do he's sure to cry.

Consequences

Use the familiar rhyme "Little Boy Blue" to open a discussion about the consequences of our actions. Help your students understand that consequences may be good or bad. Ask them to name the action taken by Little Boy Blue (he fell asleep instead of tending the sheep) and what happened as a consequence (the sheep and the cow got into places they shouldn't have been). Ask: *Was the boy in the poem acting responsibly? How do you imagine he might have felt after he woke up?*

Invite each student to imagine he or she is Little Boy Blue. Ask each child to write a page in his or her daily journal telling about the escapade in the poem. Students can embellish the story by adding other characters and telling what happened after Little Boy Blue awoke. Can they imagine further consequences? What would he do the next time he was given responsibility?

What I Do Makes a Difference

Ask your students to identify times during the schoolday when an action or event was caused by another action or event. For example, because one person interrupted another during worktime, neither child completed his work and both missed recess. Or, because one child helped another put away the math blocks during clean-up time, everyone was on time for lunch. Or, because someone left a book on the floor, someone else tripped. For each situation, contrast and compare the responsible thing to do with the irresponsible thing.

Responsibility

"Do your duty in all things. You cannot do more. You should never wish to do less."—Robert E. Lee

Take Responsibility

Your class can design and paint a mural on a large piece of colored bulletin board paper. Title the mural "Take Responsibility." Have the children illustrate and label scenes of students taking responsibility around the school. Some examples include: *I do my best work*; *I keep my desk neat*; *I do my homework on time*; *I don't litter*.

Display the mural in a prominent place, such as a hallway, for all to see and appreciate.

Excellence Is Not Perfection

A responsible person strives for excellence. Help your students understand the difference between pursuing excellence and reaching for an impossible goal—perfection. Let students know that you recognize that everyone makes mistakes, and it's okay. For example, a teacher who points out his or her own spelling error at the chalkboard will help children appreciate that even adults make mistakes. Think of the difference between excellence and perfection this way: Excellence is a process of becoming. Perfection is static. Excellence is achieved by exploring. Perfection is rigid.

Ask the children if they have ever seen a baby brother or sister who was learning to walk. Have them tell how a baby walks a few steps at a time. Just for fun, have a volunteer demonstrate. Babies drop to the floor or trip easily when they are learning, but they don't seem to mind. They get right up and try again. What would happen if a baby tried to walk, fell down, and then gave up because she couldn't do it right the first time? Would she learn to walk? Point out that when we are learning something new, we need to give ourselves a chance to make mistakes—that's how we learn. Ask children to draw a picture of a time when they were learning how to do something new.

19

Responsibility

Sharing literature increases children's understanding of character.

Literature List

These books depict role models who demonstrate responsibility to self, family, and community.

A Picture Book of Eleanor Roosevelt by David A. Adler (Holiday House, 1991). Eleanor Roosevelt accepted as her own the obligation to help the poor and minorities.

The Value of Responsibility: The Story of Ralph Bunche by Ann Donegan Johnson (Danbury Press, 1978). Ralph Bunche was a responsible world citizen, an African American who helped to establish the United Nations.

Henry David Thoreau: Walden text selections by Steve Lowe (Philomel, 1990). Thoreau's great experiment in self-reliance, his stay at Walden Pond, is depicted through excerpts of his writings and illustrated with beautiful linoleum-cut prints in this picture book.

Wilma Unlimited by Kathleen Krull (Harcourt Brace, 1996). Tells how Wilma Rudolph pursued excellence, overcoming a crippling childhood sickness to become the first American woman to win three gold medals at a single Olympics.

Paperboy

by Mary Kay Kroeger and Louise Borden (Clarion, 1996)

In this story, Willie is a paperboy who works to contribute to the family coffers. His big chance to sell a large number of papers depends on the outcome of the famous 1927 boxing match between Tunney and Dempsey. When Dempsey loses, nobody wants to buy papers in Willie's working-class neighborhood, but he dutifully mans his post anyway. The next day his supervisor rewards Willie's responsibility with a new, busier corner assignment, fit for a "champ."

Have your students work in small groups to make a list of Willie's character traits. They may come up with *hard-working, good example for his younger brother, knows what is right to do, perseveres, does his best, doesn't give up, knows and does his duty.*

Have each group write a newspaper headline that describes one of Willie's outstanding traits. For example: *Cincinnatti paperboy never gives up, wins new corner assignment.* Call on each group to give its headline after the paperboy's chant: *Extra! Extra! Read all about it!*

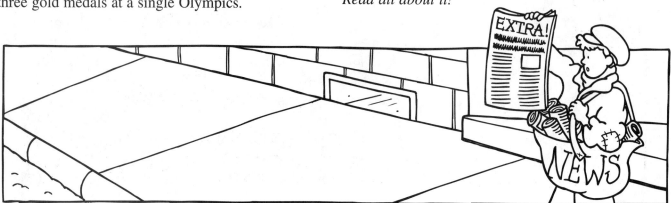

Name _____

My Responsibilities

Draw yourself in the box.
List two duties you are responsible for in each place.

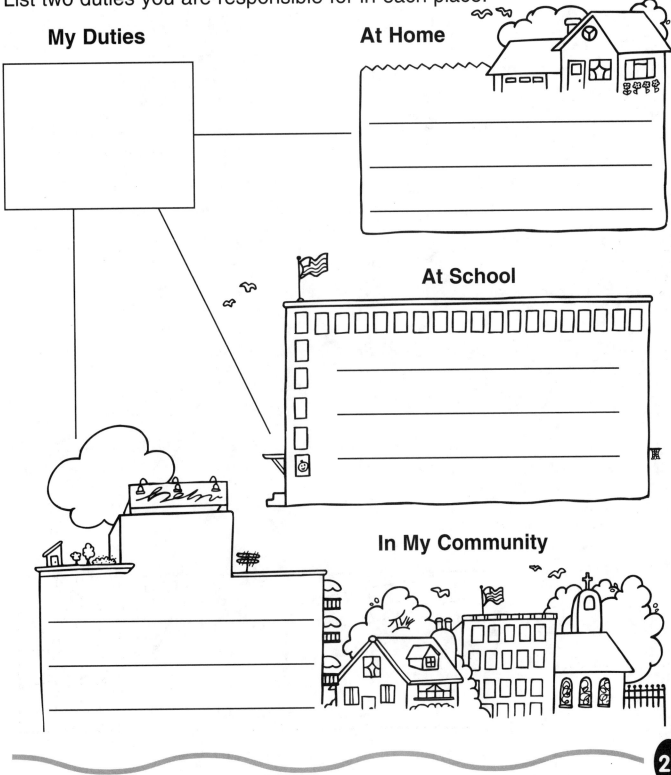

My Duties

At Home

At School

In My Community

FS119101 Developing Character When It Counts   reproducible   © Frank Schaffer Publications, Inc.

Treasure Box

Make a responsibility treasure box.
1. Find a small box with a lid.
2. Glue pasta shapes on the lid. Let it dry.
3. Paint the box.
4. Cut out the responsibility reminders.
5. Put them in your treasure box.
6. Pull out a reminder to read every day.

I do my best.

I am proud of my work.

I don't give up.

I Don't Make Excuses.

I can make a difference

I do what I am supposed to do.

I think about the consequences before I act.

I set a good example.

First Lady of the World

Read about Eleanor Roosevelt. Then color and cut out her picture and story. Glue the picture on a large sheet of paper. Draw around it to show something about Eleanor's life. Glue the story on the back.

Eleanor Roosevelt lived from 1884 to 1962. All through her life she took responsibility for making things better for people.

Eleanor had a lonely childhood. When she grew up she married Franklin Delano Roosevelt. They had six children. Her husband was crippled by polio and had to use a wheelchair. When he became governor of New York, Eleanor traveled for him, meeting the people.

Franklin was elected president in 1932. Times were hard and many people were out of work. As first lady, Eleanor worked hard planning projects to help young people, women, artists, performers, African Americans and Indians. She gave speeches about fair treatment for everyone. She also wrote for the newspapers.

After her husband died, Eleanor left the White House. But her work was not over. She became a worker for the United Nations. Leaders from all over the world met there to solve problems. At the United Nations, Eleanor worked for the rights of people everywhere.

What Is Fairness?

A fair person treats others equally, takes turns, plays by the rules, and is open-minded.

Fairness

Guide children in learning to treat one another fairly.

Making a Pledge

Fairness is an issue children may encounter many times in the school environment. Help them to establish an open, fair, and respectful classroom with a daily pledge reminder. Post a "Fairness Pledge" on chart paper and recite it together as a class when you open the day. Provide children with their own copies of the Fairness Pledge to read and sign.

Fairness Pledge
I will play by the rules.
I will take turns.
I will share.
I will try to see the other person's side.
I will be fair.

Fairness: Key Ideas

Share the following key ideas about fairness with your students. Ask for their ideas on how to apply them in the classroom.

Fairness and justice: This means to be fair and just in dealing with everyone. Treat people equally. Make decisions without playing favorites. Don't take advantage of others. Take only your fair share. Take turns and share with others.

Openness: Keep an open mind and hear people out. Listen to what others have to say before you decide. In a disagreement, try to see the other person's side. Get the facts before you make a decision.

Fairness

Share some words of wisdom with your students.

Why There Are Rules

Talk with your students about why rules and laws are important for people living together in a community. Use the following quotes and questions to begin your discussions. Make classroom banners with these quotes and others.

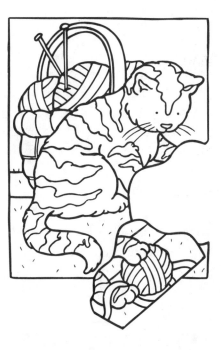

Aristotle said:

"Law is order, and good laws make for good order."

Ask: *Why is it important to have order? What makes a good law? What are some classroom rules that help us keep order?*

Hillel said:

"Do not judge your fellow man until you have stood in his place."

Ask: *Why is it important to have an open mind? Why should you have the facts before you judge someone? Were you ever judged by someone before that person had all the facts about you? How did you feel?*

Point of View

Do this activity to give children an idea of how difficult it is to see the whole picture in a situation. Ask the children to cut out magazine pictures that are interesting to them, without showing them to anyone. Then instruct each student to cut out a small part of the picture—perhaps just the cat in a picture of a family, or one tree in a park scene, or just a nose from a picture of a face. Have the students hide their pictures and only exchange the small cutout pieces. Can each student describe the whole picture in detail from just the one piece he or she was given? Explain that in making decisions we may not see the whole picture—maybe we just see a person's actions or outward appearance. It is important to get as many facts as possible and to think about different points of view in a situation.

Wise Sayings

Use the *Wise Sayings* reproducible on page 29 to introduce and discuss the meaning of some proverbs about fairness. Then have the children illustrate the true meaning of each saying.

Fairness

Cooperation or Competition?

Fairness can be a component of cooperation as well as competition. Children will most likely experience both cooperation and competition, in school as well as outside of school. Ask them to compare the two concepts, and help them to see when each one is operating.

On the board, draw a chart with two columns headed *Cooperation* and *Competition*. Ask the children to tell you where to write activities such as the following: playing in a soccer game, partcipating in a spelling bee, singing in a musical group, performing a play, being a friend, doing group work, or riding in a bike race. Ask for other ideas to add to the chart.

Cooperation	Competition
musical group	bike race
clean up time	spelling bee

Together, come up with a definition for each term. Have the children fold a large piece of drawing paper in half and write each definition on one half. Then have them illustrate each term with an example.

Taking Turns

Fairness involves taking turns. Have some fun playing a cooperative game with your students that revolves around the concept of taking turns. Here's how to play a game that is based on a Guatemalan children's game:

Set up an empty quart milk carton and gather a few playground balls. The object of the game is to touch the carton with a ball, without knocking it over. Designate a line at a reasonable distance from the carton. The first child stands at the line and rolls a ball toward the carton. The next child tries to roll his or her ball to bump the first ball closer to the carton. Each child in turn rolls a ball until the first ball touches the carton, and the game is won. If the carton is knocked over, the child who rolled the last ball begins the next game.

FS119101 Developing Character When It Counts

Fairness

Literature helps children consider issues of fairness.

Literature List

The following books can help children appreciate issues of fairness in their own lives and in the broader community.

Teammates by Peter Golenbock (Harcourt Brace Jovanovich, 1990). Jackie Robinson was the first African American to play Major League baseball. When Robinson met with racial prejudice, his white teammate Pee Wee Reese made a dramatic public gesture of support.

Spotty by Margaret Rey (Houghton Mifflin, 1997). This children's classic was first published over 50 years ago. Spotty looks different from all the other bunnies in his family and is treated unfairly.

The Value of Fairness: The Story of Nellie Bly by Ann Donegan Johnson (Danbury Press, 1977). When Nellie Bly decided to travel around the world and write about it, she was told women couldn't travel alone.

Playing Fair by Shelly Nielsen (Abdo & Daughters, 1992). Rhymes in this book deal with issues of fairness among friends, on tests, in games, and with groups.

I Am Rosa Parks

by Rosa Parks with Jim Haskins
(Dial, 1997)

This autobiographical account sheds light on the power of peaceful resistance. Rosa Parks played an integral role in the civil rights movement of the 1950s and 60s by refusing to give up her seat on a bus to a white person. This began a boycott that changed laws that were unfair to African Americans.

Discuss with your students how the unfair laws did not respect the rights of African American people. Ask the children to think about whether the laws followed the Golden Rule. Did they show tolerance for differences between people? Ask the children if they have ever experienced a time when they felt they were treated unfairly. What did they do? What else might they have done?

Fairness

How to Have a Fair Argument

Encourage your students to develop critical thinking skills and learn to debate fairly. Choose an issue with two sides for a debate. For example: Should the library be open to students during lunch recess? Have the children suggest rules of fairness for the debate, such as giving everyone a chance to speak, not interrupting when someone is speaking, being polite, and using a calm voice. Assign small groups to practice debating. Afterward, discuss as a total group how the rules of fairness worked.

Games Day

Acknowledge your students' positive behavior by rewarding them with a games day. Create an interactive display of the scales of justice on a bulletin board. On one side, use cutout numerals to display the number of gold coins that will be the class goal. Have the students "fill" the other side of the balance with gold paper coins you distribute when you observe someone demonstrating fairness or a cooperative spirit. Use a class list to monitor who has received a coin, so everyone can earn at least one. Set a goal for the number of coins needed. When the students reach their goal, they may bring in favorite board games from home and enjoy 45 minutes of playing time at the end of a designated day.

Walk a Mile in My Shoes

Discuss the meaning of the saying "Don't judge someone until you have walked a mile in his shoes." Talk about the importance of trying to see another person's side of things, and of listening to other points of view. Then have each student take off a shoe, trace it on colored construction paper, and cut it out. On the footprints, have students write what the saying means to them. Write "Walk a Mile in My Shoes" at the top of a length of bulletin board paper and have the students glue their footprints to the display.

FS119101 Developing Character When It Counts

Wise Sayings

Cut out the square. Fold on the dotted lines to make a book. Draw a picture for each saying.

It's not whether you win or lose,
it's how you play the game.

Don't judge another until you've
walked a mile in his shoes.

You can't judge a book
by its cover.

Treat others as you would
like to be treated.

What Is Caring?

A caring person shows concern for others and is charitable. A caring person is compassionate, kind, loving, and considerate.

Caring

Help your students express kindness and develop empathy and compassion for others.

Caring Words

Emphasize caring and kindness with your students. First discuss the key ideas about caring listed on this page. Then, on chart paper, list verbs of caring contributed by the children. Begin with *helping*, *understanding*, *giving*, *forgiving*, *praising*. Post this chart in a prominent spot as a reminder.

Class Journal

Start a class journal where the children can write kindnesses they observe during the day. Make the journal from large sheets of writing paper stapled between posterboard covers. Title it "Our Acts of Kindness Journal." Place the journal on a table near the "Caring Verbs" chart. Provide some special marking pens to use in the journal. Be sure that students understand they are to write about a kindness or caring thing someone else did. Share the children's journal entries at the end of the day to provide incentive and ideas for more acts of kindness.

Caring: Key Ideas

Concern for others: Show compassion and empathy. Be kind, loving, and considerate in your actions and words. Be grateful for the things people do for you, and tell them. Forgive the shortcomings of others. Don't be mean or cruel to others. Be sensitive to their feelings.

Charity: Be giving. Give your time, money, support, and comfort to make someone's life better. Do this without thinking of what you will get in return. Help people in need.

Caring

Explore concepts of kindness with poetry.

Good Deeds Come Back

In this poem, the poet tells how he unexpectedly discovered the consequences of his good actions. Read it aloud to your students.

The Arrow and the Song

I shot an arrow into the air,
It fell to earth, I knew not where;
For, so swiftly it flew, the sight
Could not follow it in its flight.

I breathed a song into the air,
It fell to earth, I knew not where;
For who has sight so keen and strong,
That it can follow the flight of song?

Long, long afterward, in an oak
I found the arrow, still unbroke;
And the song, from beginning to end,
I found again in the heart of a friend.

Henry Wadsworth Longfellow

Sharing Poetry

Share this classic poem with your students and discuss its meaning. The poet seems to be saying that by giving something from the heart (a song), the narrator found a friend. Ask: *What are some ways people can give from the heart?* (Doing something kind for someone, speaking kind words, helping someone.)

Then provide a copy of the poem (see page 36) for each child. Prepare the children for a choral reading by dividing the class into high, medium, and low voices. To do this, listen to each child recite a line. It will be fairly obvious if the voice is high or low, and the medium voices will be those remaining. Assign the low voices verse one, the high voices verse two, and medium voices verse three. Allow the groups to rehearse independently for a brief time, then rehearse the group as a whole. After a few rehearsals, challenge the children to recite their lines from memory. Finally, perform the choral reading as a gift for another class, or for parents at Open House.

FS119101 Developing Character When It Counts

Caring

Teach children that they can make a difference in the world.

Helping Hands

Encourage children to think about other people's
needs and feelings. Nurture the desire to help others
by acknowledging their contributions. Ask the
children to think of ways in which they help at home
and at school. Make a "Helping Hands" mural on a
piece of colorful bulletin board paper. Instruct each
student to trace and cut out both of their hands from
contrasting colors of construction paper. Have them
write *Home* on one and *School* on the other. Then
have them fill in the fingers with ways they help.
Glue the hands to the mural and display it.

Be a Sunflower

Spread a little sunshine in your classroom. Give your students
practice in expressing their appreciation of others. Duplicate a
paper sunflower for each child in the class, and write the child's
name on it. (See pattern, page 37.) At the beginning of the week,
distribute a paper sunflower to each child, making sure everyone
gets someone else's name. Have each child observe his or her
person during the week and think about why he or she appreciates
the person. At the end of the week, allow time for everyone to
write words of appreciation on their sunflowers. Then have one
child read what he or she wrote and give it as a gift to the child
whose name is on the sunflower. That child in turn reads what he
or she wrote and delivers it, and so on, until everyone has received
a sunflower with kind words.

Homework

Assign your students this homework: *Do something kind for
someone in your family tonight. For example, clear the dinner
dishes without being asked, bring your mom her slippers, or
help your sister straighten her bookshelf.* Give each child an
index card on which to write his or her kind deed. The
children can present the cards as their "tickets" to enter the
class the next day.

FS119101 Developing Character When It Counts

Caring

"No one is useless in this world who lightens the burden of others."—Charles Dickens

Reaching Out to Others

Children can make a difference in their communities by reaching out to others in their families and neighborhoods. Encourage your students to look for ways to help others. Maybe they can make regular visits to an elderly relative, take out the trash for Dad, spruce up the school by planting flowers, or bake cookies for a neighbor who is feeling under the weather. Once children begin to look for ways to show kindness to others, they will find a myriad of opportunities.

Begin a chain reaction of kindness by challenging your students to hang a "chain of good deeds" around the classroom. As each one performs an act of kindness, he or she can add a paper link to the chain. Provide precut strips of construction paper for the children to write their good deeds on. Encourage them to add to the chain daily. How many times can they make the chain go around the classroom?

Help for the Homeless

Children can make a difference in the community by helping the homeless. Enlist parents to help with this project. Children can assemble packets of useful items in gallon-size zipper-lock plastic bags and donate them to a homeless shelter or soup kitchen. Ask parents to help by donating toiletries in sample sizes (toothpaste, shampoo, soap), new combs, nail clippers, toothbrushes, packets of gum, small notepads, and other small items. Have the children pack the items into individual zipper-lock bags and decorate them with seasonal stickers. Children may wish to add friendly notes and sign their first names.

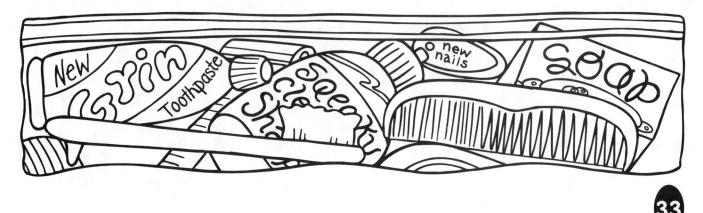

FS119101 Developing Character When It Counts

Caring

Use literature to encourage your students to think of others.

Literature List

The following books can help children learn the value of caring for others.

Androcles and the Lion an Aesop fable adapted by Janet Stevens (Holiday House, 1989). Androcles, the runaway slave, helps a wounded lion and is unexpectedly repaid for his kindness. He learns that a noble soul never forgets a kindness.

Mufaro's Beautiful Daughters by John Steptoe (Lothrop, Lee & Shepard, 1987). Mufaro sends his two beautiful daughters—one ill-tempered and one kind—to meet the king, who is looking for a wife.

A Picture Book of Florence Nightingale by David Adler (Holiday House, 1992). Florence Nightingale dedicated her life to helping the poor and sick. Her work changed the nursing profession.

Chicken Soup for Little Souls: The Best Night Out With Dad adapted by Lisa McCourt (Health Communications, 1997). Danny meets a younger boy while waiting in line to buy tickets to the circus. When things don't go right the younger boy suffers disappointment—until Danny makes a charitable gesture.

More Than Anything Else

by Marie Bradby
(Orchard, 1995)

In this powerful story, young Booker T. Washington works long hours at the saltworks, shoveling salt. But his dream is to learn to read. One day he meets a man who takes the time to teach Booker how to unlock the mystery of the marks that reveal the secrets Booker hungers to know.

Ask the children if they can remember a time before they could read. Who taught them how to begin reading? Can they think of other things they were eager to learn to do (play baseball, ride a bike, knit)? Who helped them learn? Help children appreciate that those who teach others show their kindness and caring.

Invite the children to help you make a list of caring professions. Ask what types of workers they know who care for others (teachers, doctors, nurses, social workers, paramedics, firefighters). Have them paint a mural on butcher paper showing some of those occupations. Title the mural "We Care, We Help."

Caring

Develop a caring atmosphere in the classroom.

Coin-a-Day

Teach your students that a caring person is charitable. One way to do this is by celebrating National UNICEF Month in October. UNICEF is the United Nations Children's Fund. Contributions to the fund help children in developing countries.

UNICEF suggests inviting each child in the class to bring in a coin every day from home. The children will be able to see how even a small contribution, when combined with those of others, makes an important difference. You can write to the address above, or to your local field office, for further information and more ideas on how to participate.

U.S. Committee for UNICEF
National Headquarters
333 East 38th Street
New York, New York 10016
212-686-5522

www.supportunicef.org

Spreading Cheer

Involve your students in painting posters for the lobby of a local hospital, nursing home facility, or senior citizen center. Have the children choose cheerful and inspiring messages to illustrate.

Class Motto

Ask your students to think of suggestions for a class motto that would reflect a kind and caring classroom, such as *We care and we show it!* or *A classroom is a caring place*. Take a vote to decide which one to adopt, and then have the children create a banner with their motto. Display it above the chalkboard. Encourage the practice of writing the class motto at the top of the first paper the children write each day.

FS119101 Developing Character When It Counts

The Arrow and the Song
by Henry Wadsworth Longfellow

Low
Voices

I shot an arrow into the air,
It fell to earth, I knew not where;
For, so swiftly it flew, the sight
Could not follow it in its flight.

High
Voices

I breathed a song into the air,
It fell to earth, I knew not where;
For who has sight so keen and strong,
That it can follow the flight of song?

Medium
Voices

Long, long afterward, in an oak
I found the arrow, still unbroke;
And the song, from beginning to end,
I found again in the heart of a friend.

reproducible   FS119101 Developing Character When It Counts

Sunflower

Write a nice message on the sunflower. Cut it out and give it to a classmate.

Dear _____,

You are a ray of sunshine.
I appreciate you because

_____

_____

_____

_____

_____

FS119101 Developing Character When It Counts   reproducible   © Frank Schaffer Publications, Inc.

Acts of Kindness

A person of character looks for the kind and caring thing to do or say. Read each situation and think about what could be done. Then write your answer to the child who is speaking.

My friend Paul and I both entered an art contest at the grocery store. Paul won first prize—a new bike. What should I say?

_____
_____
_____
_____

At school, Hattie has a cold and needs a tissue. She doesn't have one. What should I do?

_____
_____
_____
_____

Alan is crying because he lost a book he brought to school to share. What should I say?

_____
_____
_____
_____

My friend dropped her lunch money just when the school bus got here to pick us up. What should I do?

_____
_____
_____

Citizenship

Guide your students to becoming good citizens.

Reading About Citizenship

Introduce your students to the concept of citizenship with a discussion of the key ideas listed on this page. Have the students reflect on what their responsibilities are as citizens of your classroom, your school, your community, and the world.

Set up a citizenship book display in a corner of your classroom. Provide books about people who were outstanding citizens and contributed to their communities. Some examples are: Paul Revere, Rachel Carson, Frederick Douglass, Eleanor Roosevelt, and Ralph Bunche. Each day for a week, read aloud from one of the books and talk about the contributions made by the subject or main character. Also allow the children time to read the books with a partner.

Cooperative Book Report

One way to promote good citizenship is by encouraging your students to work cooperatively. Assign them to work in small groups of four children. Have them take turns reading aloud one of the books from the display to the people in their group. Then give each group a copy of the *Cooperative Book Report* on page 44. Groups should divide the work among themselves so that one child is the reader, one the writer, one the discussion leader, and one the artist. Have the readers share their group's completed reports with the class.

Citizenship: Key Ideas

Do your share: Be a good neighbor and a good citizen. Contribute to the common good. Volunteer to make things cleaner, safer, and better. Protect the environment. Speak up to make things better.

Respect authority and law: Play by the rules. Follow the laws. Obey parents and teachers.

What Is Citizenship?

Good citizens do their share, contribute to their communities, obey rules and laws, respect authority, and cooperate with others.

Citizenship

"Service is the rent we pay for living. It is the very purpose of life and not something you do in your spare time."—Marian Wright Edelman

Artifact Kits

Introduce children to the lives of people who exemplify good citizenship. Invite the children to select books about outstanding citizens from the classroom book corner or from the school library. The assignment is to read the book in order to learn as much about the outstanding citizen as possible. Then each student can make an "artifact kit" about the person he or she read about and present it to the class.

To make the kit, students can use brown paper grocery bags. They can put clue items inside of the bags. For example, for Rachel Carson, the artifact kit might include a children's magazine (Rachel won a prize for writing for one when she was young), a toy fish (she worked for the U.S. Bureau of Fisheries), and a seashell (for her book *The Sea Around Us*). The children should also put their books inside the "kits", then label the bags with their own names. When it is a child's turn to present to the class, he or she can take out one artifact at a time and explain its significance while talking about the outstanding citizen.

Good Citizens Are Everywhere

As homework, ask each student to find and clip a newspaper article about someone who is a good citizen. With help from a parent or other adult, the student can use a yellow crayon to highlight the important facts that tell why the person is a good citizen. The children can share their news clippings with the class, then post them on a bulletin board.

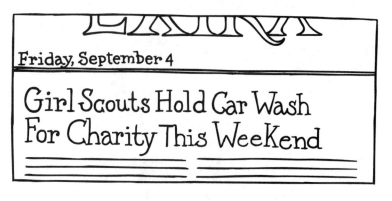

Fairy Tale Citizens

Have some fun with the concept of citizenship. Ask your students to think of fairy tale characters who could be considered good citizens because they helped someone in trouble, obeyed the law, or contributed to their community in some way. For example, the elves who helped the shoemaker in "The Elves and the Shoemaker," the woodcutter who saved Little Red Riding Hood, or the third little pig who sheltered his brothers. Provide books of fairy tales and other stories for children to browse through. Then have each child select a character and complete the "newspaper article" form on page 45.

Citizenship

"In all ways and at all times people have a need for sharing life with others and the search for community."—Virginia Hamilton

Making a Contribution

Artists of all kinds make very special contributions to their communities. Discuss with your students ways in which artists do this. (They create works of art such as statues, murals, buildings, songs, dances, and symphonies that symbolize the hopes and dreams of many people. Their work may remind people of the important things we all have in common.)

Make a class scrapbook of works of art that the children find appealing. Invite the children to share postcards of buildings and monuments, song lyrics and poems about making the world a better place, and their own drawings and writings. Make the scrapbook an ever-growing collection and keep it in the classroom library for all to appreciate.

The More We Get Together

Making music together encourages children to pool their talents and teaches them about their responsibilities to the larger group. Develop a sense of community in your classroom by having regular sing-a-longs. Any songs that are fun to sing together will do, or choose some songs about living together as a community. Here's a list to get you started:

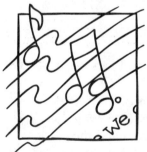

The More We Get Together
This Land Is Your Land
It's a Small World
What a Wonderful World
One Light, One Sun

Our Community Songbook

Make class books using the lyrics of any of the above songs. Give each child a sheet of drawing paper. Divide up the lyrics and write each phrase on a sheet of colored construction paper. These will serve as page dividers in the book. Then assign each child a phrase to illustrate on a sheet of drawing paper. (Some phrases may be illustrated by more than one child.) Assemble the divider pages, with the children's drawings between them, to make a book. Add posterboard covers. Display the book at Open House with a cassette recording of the children singing the song.

Citizenship

Citizenship includes caring for the environment.

Our Environment

Encourage your students to care for the environment and share their ideas with others. Volunteer to have your class decorate a bulletin board for a hall or the school office. Cover the board in light blue paper and have the children cut out grass and flowers to attach along the bottom of the board. Title the board "Taking Care of Earth Is Everyone's Job." Recycle copy paper that has been used on one side by cutting it in half. Have the children use the unprinted side to write a suggestion they have tried for recycling or caring for the environment. For example, *I sit near a window to read instead of turning on a light* or *I asked my parents if I could plant a tree for my birthday*. Post the suggestions on the bulletin board to share with others in the school.

Posters for the Environment

Make a study of the environment with your class. Help students discover environmental problems and what can be done about them. Share books about nature and preserving the environment. Then have students design posters. Have each child select an environmental problem or solution to feature on the poster. Explain that the purpose of the poster is to motivate others to care for the environment. Then encourage the children to take their posters home and enlist the aid of a family member in finding a public place where it can be hung. They might ask at a local grocery store, or at city hall, or Mom or Dad might post it at work.

Universal Passport

Explain to students that they are citizens of many places at once: the universe, Earth, their country, state, city, school, and classroom. Make copies of *Passport to the Universe* on page 46. Have students fill in the passport, cut it apart, and staple it into a booklet.

Citizenship

Use literature to help children answer the call of citizenship.

Literature List

Come Back, Salmon by Molly Cone (Sierra Club, 1992). This book tells the true story of a group of elementary school children who adopted a creek and brought it back to life.

Just a Dream by Chris Van Allsburg (Houghton Mifflin, 1990). Walter doesn't do his part to keep the environment clean, until he has a dream that takes him to the future.

Kate Shelley and the Midnight Express by Margaret K. Wetterer (Carolrhoda, 1990). Kate's story is true. It tells how she saved lives in a heavy storm that took out a railroad bridge.

One Giant Leap: The Story of Neil Armstrong by Don Brown (Houghton Mifflin, 1998). This picture book biography tells the story of the first man to walk on the moon.

Paul Revere's Ride by Henry Wadsworth Longfellow. Illustrated by Ted Rand (Dutton, 1990). The famous verse tells the story of the silversmith who warned the Americans that the British were coming.

Sweet Clara and the Freedom Quilt by Deborah Hopkinson (Knopf, 1993). Clara is a young slave who sews a map into a quilt. She leaves it behind for others to follow when she escapes to freedom.

Miss Rumphius

by Barbara Cooney
(Viking, 1982)

Miss Rumphius plants lupines, making the world more beautiful. Have the children brainstorm ways of making the world more beautiful. Write their suggestions on sentence strips. Have them paint a large Earth with poster paint on white butcher paper. Trim around it and mount it on a blue background. Post the sentence strips around the Earth. Title the display "We Are Earth's Citizens."

FS119101 Developing Character When It Counts

Name _____

Cooperative Book Report

People in Our Group: _____

Book Title: _____

Author: _____

In this book, who showed good citizenship?

_____

How did this person show good citizenship?

_____

_____

What did you learn about citizenship from this book?

_____

_____

Here is a picture about the book.

```
┌─────────────────────────────────────────────────┐
│                                                 │
│                                                 │
│                                                 │
│                                                 │
│                                                 │
│                                                 │
│                                                 │
└─────────────────────────────────────────────────┘
```

Name _____

The Fairy Tale News

Draw a picture for the *Fairy Tale News*. Show a fairy tale character or other storybook character who was a good citizen. Write a caption for your picture. The caption should answer these questions:

  1. **Who** is the character?
  2. **What** is happening in the picture?
  3. **Why** was the character a good citizen?

_____

_____

_____

_____

Passport to the Universe

in the state of

_____

in the city of

_____

This certifies that

_____

(name)

is a citizen of the Universe,

at _____ School,

Room _____

on planet _____,

in the country of

_____

and has all the rights and responsibilities of citizenship.

Signed _____

reproducible